Hotel &
Resort
INTERIORS

WITHDRAWN

ROCKPORT
PUBLISHERS

First published in the United States of America by:
Rockport Publishers, Inc.
33 Commercial Street
Gloucester, Massachusetts 01930-5089
Telephone: (978) 282-9590
Facsimile: (978) 283-2742

Distributed to the book trade and art trade in the United States by:
North Light Books, an imprint of
F & W Publications
1507 Dana Avenue
Cincinnati, Ohio 45207
Telephone: (800) 289-0963

Other Distribution by:
Rockport Publishers, Inc.
Gloucester, Massachusetts 01930-5089

ISBN 1-56496-484-1

10 9 8 7 6 5 4 3 2 1

Designer: SYP Design & Production
Cover Image credits: see page 63

Printed in China

Introduction

How does one choose the hotel or resort destination that feels "right"? It's a simple matter of design. The design of a hotel removes a guest from their day-to-day existence, and can create the impression of living in a different time and place. The romance of a Renaissance villa, an eighteenth-century palace, or a rustic Wild West lodge are all attainable; for a few days or weeks, one may choose a place where a deeply held fantasy—of luxury, image, or aspiration—can be fulfilled.

In urban settings, hotels often create an insulated, world-of-their-own haven that muffles the noise and activity of the street with heavy drapes, calm colors, and low lights. At a destination resort, on the other hand, beautiful surroundings are part of the allure, and dictate a more open feeling. And then there's the choice of amenities: a luxurious spa, well-appointed fitness area, pool, piano bar, or world-class restaurant can add immeasurably to a guest's stay. Top it all off with room service—what could be better?

Design AiGroup/Architects, P.C.
Project The Peninsula Hotel, Hotel Lobby
NEW YORK, NEW YORK

Part of a $50 million historic renovation, the elegant lobby reflects a successful marriage between Art Nouveau and Classic Beaux Arts styling.

PHOTO: JAIME ARDILES-ARCE

Design Aiello Associates, Inc.
Project Bullwhackers Gaming Establishment
CENTRAL CITY, COLORADO

View down the stairs from the restaurant.

PHOTO: ED LACASSE

Design Cheryl Rowley Interior Design
Project Hotel Monaco
SAN FRANCISCO, CALIFORNIA

Classical Greek architecture, rich saturated
Mediterranean colors, and exotic furniture all
inspire thoughts of journeys afar at the Hotel
Monaco, San Francisco.

PHOTO: COURTESY OF CHERYLN ROWLEY INTERIOR DESIGN

Design Candra Scott
Int. Architect Candra Scott and
The Malder Company
Architect Candra Scott
Lighting Candra Scott
Project The Governor Hotel
PORTLAND, OREGON

The lobby area features a larger-than-life size mural of Lewis and Clark's journey from Celilo Falls down the Columbia to Fort Clatsop, and Sacajawea overlooking the ocean as she saw it for the first time. Custom designed furniture with hand-painted feather and diamond motifs, taken from the original architectural details, continues this theme in the 100 guest rooms. Leaf patterns decorate both the column-based standing lamps and massive, hanging fixtures.

PHOTO: LANGDON CLAY

Design Candra Scott
Int. Architect Candra Scott and
The Malder Company
Architect Candra Scott
Lighting Candra Scott
Project The Governor Hotel
PORTLAND, OREGON

The artwork for the guestrooms was inspired by Lewis and Clark's journal illustrating nature, flora, and fauna. Each guest room door is appointed with an Indian wall sconce, which throws a romantic "torch" light. Painted feather and diamond motifs, taken from the original architectural details, continues this theme in the one hundred guest rooms. Leaf patterns decorate both the column-based standing lamps and massive hanging fixtures.

PHOTO: LANGDON CLAY

Design Babey-Moulton, Inc.
Architect Moore Ruble Yudell
Project Plaza Las Fuentes Hotel
PASADENA, CALIFORNIA

Massive hanging chandeliers dominate the
aesthetics of this passage, providing the general
illumination and on intriguing design elements.
Seating groups are each in the warm light of a
large table lamp. Lit upper balconies create
definition and add perspective to the space.

PHOTO: JAIME ARDILES, ARCE

Design Rita St. Clair Associates, Inc.
Project Doubletree Inn at the Colonnade
BALTIMORE, MARYLAND

Flame maple paneling and silk wallcovering were inspired by the Swedish Beidemeier sofa. Lobby is further defined by octagonal area rug and circular ceiling coffer opening up to a trompe l'oeil sky.

PHOTO: MAXWELL MACKENZIE

Design Rita St. Clair Associates, Inc.
Project Doubletree Inn at the Colonnade
BALTIMORE, MARYLAND

Wood panel details flow around the granite capped registration desk. Etched bronze elevator door panels repeat the elliptical motif.

PHOTO: MAXWELL MACKENZIE

Design Rita St. Clair Associates, Inc.
Project The Palmer House Hilton, Red Lacquer Room
CHICAGO, ILLINOIS

Red luminous wall glazing adds drama to this room with gilded panel moldings. The cream and gilt cove and ceiling and gold draperies impart elegance and freshness in contrast to the rich palette.

PHOTO: WAYNE CABLE

Design Dow/Fletcher
Project Best Western Icicle Inn, Lobby
LEAVENWORTH, WASHINGTON

Design Cheryl Rowley Interior Design
Project Hotel Monaco
SAN FRANCISCO, CALIFORNIA

Free-spirited public spaces and fantastical guest
rooms give form to Rowley's vision of the Hotel
Monaco as an exploring ship, having plied the
farthest oceans of the world for treasures, now
at rest and swelled with its booty.

PHOTO: COURTESY OF CHERYL ROWLEY INTERIOR DESIGN

Design Cheryl Rowley Interior Design
Project Hotel Monaco
SAN FRANCISCO, CALIFORNIA

Classical Greek architecture, rich saturated
Mediterranean colors, and exotic furniture all
inspire thoughts of journeys afar at the Hotel
Monaco, San Francisco.

PHOTO: COURTESY OF CHERYL ROWLEY INTERIOR DESIGN

Design Candra Scott
Int. Architect Candra Scott
Lighting Paul Marantz, Kaoru Mende
Project The Manhattan
CHIBA, JAPAN

The interior decoration of the hospitality suites differs from suite to suite, each named after a celebrity and capturing a moment from a classic movie. The Humphrey Bogart suite is in a tailored 1940s style, paneled in deep rich tones of mahogany. Period sconces give the room an intimate atmosphere, while recessed spotlights and sculptural pendants provide abundant task light for conferences.

PHOTO: YOSHITERU BABA

Design Di Leonardo International, Inc.
Project New World Hotel
KOWLOON, HONG KONG

For the renovation of the New World Hotel in Kowloon, Hong Kong, additional area above the lobby, was secured to created a dramatic two-volume space. A modern escalator becomes a design element, connecting the lobby to a lower meeting level.

PHOTO: DIMENSIONS MAGAZINE PHOTOGRAPHER

Design Candra Scott
Int. Architect Candra Scott
Lighting Paul Marantz, Kaoru Mende
Project The Manhattan
CHIBA, JAPAN

The lobby combines original Art Deco lighting and
furniture, as well as luxurious custom designed
pieces from the 1925 Paris exhibition. The rich
palette of soft greens, golds, and reds creates a
feeling of warmth and comfort. Recessed spot
lighting strengthens the illusion that light is streaming
from the painting on the wall. Dramatic uplighting
enhances architectural features.

PHOTO: YOSHITERU BABA

Design Hill/Glazier Architects
Project Hyatt Regency Hill Country Resort
SAN ANTONIO, TEXAS

The 575-room Hyatt Regency Hill Country Resort in San Antonio, Texas, has traditional limestone facades, wood porches, and other typically Texas Territorial-style features. Two massive stone fireplaces welcome guests to the lobby.

Design Knauer, Inc.
Project Grand Geneva Resort And Spa
LAKE GENEVA, WISCONSIN

This Lake Geneva, Wisconsin resort was entirely revitalized within twelve months. In a bold move, the lobby was relocated from a tiny inconspicuous space to what was previously the indoor pool, to take full advantage of the magnificent view.

PHOTO: JAMES YOCHUM

Design Media Five Limited
Project Yokohama New Grand
Inter-Continental Hotel
YOKOHAMA, JAPAN

PHOTO: MANNY HABRON, RON STARR, AND COURTESY
OF THE HOTEL

Design Rita St. Clair Associates, Inc.
Project The Palmer House Hilton
CHICAGO, ILLINOIS

Garden murals by artist Joseph Sheppard fill
architectural niches and create a pavilion-like
effect for the State Ballroom. Faux marble
pilasters and glazed finishes delineate the
ornate moldings.

Design Elias Design Group, Inc.
Project The Jefferson Hotel, The Atrium
RICHMOND, VIRGINIA

This historically certified property was restored to its original grandeur with marbleized columns finished in the old scagiola method. The Grand Stair served as the model for Tara in "Gone with the Wind."

PHOTO: WHITNEY COX

Design Elias Design Group, Inc.
Project The Jefferson Hotel,
Signature Restaurant
RICHMOND, VIRGINIA

Recessed low voltage lighting, hand woven rugs, and contemporary etched glass are blended with the architectural elements in this historically certified property to create a dramatic introduction to his fine dining experience.

PHOTO: WHITNEY COX

Design Elias Design Group, Inc.
Project The Sheraton Carlton, Presidential
Suite Bedroom
WASHINGTON, D.C.

This elegant, award-winning bedroom, belies its
security systems complete with bullet-proof glass
an adjacent guard facilities required by its location
near the Capitol.

PHOTO: PETER PAIGE

Design Elias Design Group, Inc.
Project The Sheraton Carlton, Presidential Suite
Dining Room
WASHINGTON, D.C.

Document wallcovering and reproduction
American 1800's period furniture reflect the
hotel's location two blocks from the nation's
Capitol building.

PHOTO: PETER PAIGE

Design Elias Design Group, Inc.
Project The Sheraton Carlton, Guestroom
WASHINGTON, D.C.

Furnishings were custom designed for these luxury guestrooms which were awarded the Gold Key for Excellence in design by the American Hotel and Motel Association.

PHOTO: PETER PAIGE

Design Cooper Carry, Inc.
Project Norwalk Waterside Convention Center & Marriott Hotel
NORFOLK, VIRGINIA

The 110,000 sq. ft. conference facility has a 15,000 sq. ft. exhibit hall, two ballrooms, and additional meeting spaces Transparency at the entry helps advertise the buildings exhibits.

Design Pamela Temples Interiors, Inc.
Project Hyatt Regency Grand Cypress
ORLANDO, FLORIDA

The villas of Grand Cypress greet guests with a warm color palette and cozy furniture in tranquil surroundings.

PHOTO: ROBERT STARLING

Design Barry Design Associates, Inc.
Project Imperial Hotel Osaka
OSAKA, JAPAN

Challenged to maintain references to the original design of the architectural visionary Frank Lloyd Wright, the designers established a radial floor patterning when renovating the atrium that is interwoven with sub-patterns reflecting the original surrounding windows.

Design Barry Design Associates, Inc.
Project Hotel Nikko Tokyo
TOKYO, JAPAN

A calm and elegant seating area off the main lobby continues the them of light colors.

Design Barry Design Associates, Inc.
Project Imperial Hotel Osaka
OSAKA, JAPAN

The Imperial Suite is the sometimes home of the Crown Prince of Japan. From its granite, anigre, and marble bathroom, to its rich-colored living-room furnishings, to the "men's club" look of the wood-paneled library, this suite, like the hotel, is world class.

Design Arrowstreet, Inc.
Project Harvard Square Hotel
CAMBRIDGE, MASSACHUSETTS

This hotel conference center was created from a dilapidated historic building protected by the Boston Landmarks Commission. The gutted shell now houses 20,000 square feet of presentation and meeting space.

Design Hughes Design Associates
Project Four Seasons Hotel
PHILADELPHIA, PENNSYLVANIA

The updated lobby and guestrooms of the Four
Seasons Hotel, Philadelphia, are elegantly
appointed with rich textiles and furnishings.

Design Hughes Design Associates
Project Capital Hilton
WASHINGTON, D.C.

One of Washington, DC.'s more prominent
hotels, the Capital Hilton was recently refurbished
by Hughes.

Design Hughes Design Associates
Project Capital Hilton
WASHINGTON, D.C.

Part of the ITT Luxury Collection, The Carlton's
guest rooms and suites were given classical,
elegant updates. Hughes also refurbished the tea
lounge, ballroom terrace, and meeting rooms.

Design Knauer Inc.
Project Milwaukee Hilton
MILWAUKEE, WISCONSIN

The grand staircase joining the ballrooms was uncovered and restored according to Holabird and Roche's original details. The rich colors and elegance of the original design are revealed in the ballrooms and guest rooms.

PHOTO: JAMES YOCHUM

Design Elias Design Group, Inc.
Project The Richmond Airport Hilton, Corridor
RICHMOND, VIRGINIA

Public corridors provide continuity to the Frank
Lloyd Wright influence experienced upon
entering the hotel.

PHOTO: PETER PAIGE

Design Vivian/Nichols Associates, Inc.
Project Doubletree Hotel/Park West, Lobby Bar
DALLAS, TEXAS

Design Brennan Beer Gorman/Architects
Brennan Beer Gorman Monk/Interiors
Project Crowne Plaza
WASHINGTON, D.C.

The fifteen-million-dollar renovation of this
historic Beaux Arts building in Washington, D.C.,
includes a new scalloped-glass canopy that
harmonizes with the decorative exterior elements,
yet still respects the integrity of the original facade.
The barrel-vaulted ceiling inside the lobby closely
resembles its original splendor.

PHOTO: DAN CUNNINGHAM

Design Birch Coffey Design Associates, Inc.
Project The Mercury

The circular layout and flow of the café eating areas assure comfortable and efficient passenger service on the Century, one of Celebrity Cruises' newest luxury liners.

PHOTO: PHILLIP ENNIS

Design Elias Design Group, Inc.
Project The Richmond Airport Hilton, Lobby
RICHMOND, VIRGINIA

The entrance seating group exhibits a contemporary Frank Lloyd Wright flavor which the designer incorporated into the interiors to reflect the architect's treatment of the building's exterior.

PHOTO: PETER PAIGE

Design Design Continuum, Inc.
Project Hotel Inter-Continental
LOS ANGELES, CALIFORNIA

The elegance of the lobby of the Hotel Inter-Continental Los Angeles is softly modern and very inviting, with contemporary artworks on permanent display.

PHOTO: MILROY & MCALLEER

Design AiGroup/Architects, P.C.
Project Radisson Plaza Hotel at Kalamazoo Center, Websters Restaurant & Bar
KALAMAZOO, MICHIGAN

Leaded glass, a featured wine collection, marble floors and rich mahogany millwork highlight this elegant 80 seat dinner atmosphere.

PHOTO: GARY KNIGHT & ASSOCIATES

Design Aiello Associates, Inc.
Project Poco Diablo Resort
SEDONA, ARIZONA

The Furnace Creek Inn Resort in California makes use of regional materials and local design aesthetics to create comfortable environments.

PHOTO: PHILLIP NILSSON

Design Simon Martin - Vegue Winkelstein Moris
Architect Ward Young Architects
Lighting Bradley A. Bouch, Jim Benya, Luminae
Souter Lighting Design
Project Resort at Squaw Creek
SQUAW CREEK, CALIFORNIA

Entering the lobby, the indoor space echoes
nature's colors on a warmer, more human scale.
The designers underscored the inherent opulence
of the natural materials, which include flame
granite in the floors, granite boulders taken from
the site, and wrought-hewn Douglas fir framed
chairs. Recessed spotlights create sculptural
shadows on the massive stone columns, while
hanging fixtures create pools of light to lead
patrons toward the information desk.

PHOTO: CHARLES MCGRATH

Design Aiello Associates, Inc.
Project Furnace Creek Inn Resort
DEATH VALLEY, CALIFORNIA

The Furnace Creek Inn Resort in California
makes use of regional materials and local design
aesthetics to create comfortable environments.

PHOTO: CHAD SLATTERY

Design Cheryl Rowley Interior Design
Project Hotel Monaco
SAN FRANCISCO, CALIFORNIA

Free-spirited public spaces and fantastical guest
rooms give form to Rowley's vision of the Hotel
Monaco as an exploring ship, having plied the
farthest oceans of the world for treasures, now at
rest and swelled with its booty.

PHOTO: COURTESY OF CHERYL ROWLEY INTERIOR DESIGN

Design Parisi
Project Villas of Renaissance
LA JOLLA, CALIFORNIA

The rotunda at the Villas of Renaissance is filled
with natural light.

PHOTO: ED GOHLICH

Design Cheryl Rowley Interior Design
Project Beverly Prescott Hotel, Living Room
LOS ANGELES, CALIFORNIA

Design Cheryl Rowley Interior Design
Project Beverly Prescott Hotel
LOS ANGELES, CALIFORNIA

Rich colors of coral, rose, and cream combine
with mahogany and cherry woods in the hotel's
ten suites.

Design Texeira, Inc.
Project Regent Beverly Wilshire
BEVERLY HILLS, CALIFORNIA

Design The Gettys Group, Inc.
Project Radisson Hotel and Suites
CHICAGO, ILLINOIS

The nine-million dollar renovation of the Radisson
Hotel in Chicago was finished within a year, with
the hotel remaining open throughout the process.

PHOTO: JOHN MILLER / HEDRICH BLESSING PHOTOGRAPHY

Design Barry Design Associates, Inc.
Project Hotel Nikko Tokyo
TOKYO, JAPAN

The living room of the Presidential Suite focuses
on the vistas of the surrounding bay. Soft
earth-tones, minimal patterns, and luxe fabrics
offer a sense of openness and calm that is
decidedly Oriental.

Design Arrowstreet, Inc.
Project Harvard Square Hotel
CAMBRIDGE, MASSACHUSETTS

Design Design Continuum, Inc.
Project Hotel Inter-Continental
LOS ANGELES, CALIFORNIA

Mixed genres in the public spaces and the
California-style suits all add up to the
West Coast comfort.

PHOTO: MILROY & MCALLEER

Design Passanella & Klein Stolzman & Berg
Architects
Project Mansfield Hotel
NEW YORK, NEW YORK

Beautiful details of the original building were
recaptured throughout the hotel.

Design Peter Gisolfi Associates
Project Castle at Tarrytown
TARRYTOWN, NEW YORK

Each of the guest suites were individually designed and furnished.

PHOTO: NORMAN MCGRATH

Design Aiello Associates, Inc.
Project Embassy Suites, Atrium
DENVER, COLORADO

PHOTO: PHILLIP NILSSON

Design Victor Huff Partnership
Project Society Center Marriott,
Executive Board Room
CLEVELAND, OHIO

Design Vivian/Nichols Associates, Inc.
Project Houstonian Hotel and
Conference Center
HOUSTON, TEXAS

A reference to the atmosphere of a turn-of-the-
century great lodge creates an understated
mountain environment, replete with natural
materials, warm colors, and commissioned nature
and country artwork at the Houstonian Hotel and
Conference Center.

PHOTO: MICHAEL FRENCE

Design Janet Gay Freed
Architect G.K. Muennig
Lighting Linda Ferry
Project Post Ranch Inn

The design team's challenge for the Post Ranch Inn was to make each room a private, intimate retreat. The light sources had to blend with the highly unique architecture, but not detract from the spectacular Pacific Ocean views. The majority of the room's light is ambient, created by several custom designed incandescent uplights. The uplights reflect lift off a sculptural, curved wood ceiling, drawing out the natural tones of the wood. Low-voltage cable lights provide accent light. Three swing-arm lamps serve as reading lights for the bed and seating.

PHOTO: DOUGLAS SALIN

Design Dow/Fletcher
Project Edgewater Hotel
SEATTLE, WASHINGTON

Lobby of downtown waterfront hotel

Design Studio Sofield, Inc.
Project Soho Grand
NEW YORK, NEW YORK

The historical, industrial theme is referred to
throughout. Even the contemporary elegance of
the guest rooms is punctuated with Stickley-era
type furniture and furnishings.

43

Design Vivian/Nichols Associates, Inc.
Project Westchase Hilton
HOUSTON, TEXAS

Commanding three guest-room bays and the
penthouse, the Presidential Suite of the
Westchase Hilton lends itself to business functions
as well as an urban retreat.

PHOTO: MICHAEL FRENCE

Design Peter Gisolfi Associates
Project Castle at Tarrytown
TARRYTOWN, NEW YORK

Much of the interiors were recreated by Gisolfi,
including elaborate interior finishes and details.

PHOTO: NORMAN MCGRATH

Design HLW International
Project La Palestra
NEW YORK, NEW YORK

The once grand old ballroom of the Hotel Des Artistes in Manhattan was transformed by HLW International into La Palestra Center for Preventative Medicine, which is a cross between a physical fitness and medical fitness facility. Many elements of the ballroom's gracious grandeur were restored.

PHOTO: SCOTT FRANCES

Design HLW International
Project The Barbizon Hotel
NEW YORK, NEW YORK

Design HLW International
Project La Palestra
NEW YORK, NEW YORK

New elements at La Palestra were carefully
inserted into the shell. These include ribbed-
wood ceilings, warm steel walls, and a gallery of
mirrors under the sky-light. Their purpose is to
delineate different scales and different activities,
with patient support areas, technical offices, and
consultation rooms organized around the main
treatment areas.

PHOTO: SCOTT FRANCES

Design Parisi
Project Mirada Hospitality Center
RANCHO MIRAGE, CALIFORNIA

The Mirada at the Ritz Carlton exhibits rich
details, although in very different styles.

PHOTO: PETER MALINOWSKI

Design Pasanella & Klein Stolzman & Berg
Architects
Project Mansfield Hotel
NEW YORK, NEW YORK

Ornate ceilings were preserved throughout the hotel.

PHOTO: MICHAEL MORAN

Design Pasanella & Klein Stolzman & Berg Architects
Project Franklin Hotel
NEW YORK, NEW YORK

In the transformation from a rundown crack house to a high-design but low-budget hotel, the designers used low-cost materials for custom-designed furnishings, repeating the use of tubular steel frames and cherry plywood throughout.

PHOTO: CHUCK CHOI

Design Pamela Temples Interiors, Inc.
Project Buena Vista Palace
BUENA VISTA, FLORIDA

Refreshing colors create a serene atmosphere at the Spa of the Buena Vista Palace.

PHOTO: MICHAEL LOWRY PHOTOGRAPHY &
ROBERT STARLING PHOTOGRAPHY

Design The Gettys Group, Inc.

Project Hilton Inn Lisle

NAPERVILLE, ILLINOIS

Sophisticated interiors make this renovated
suburban hotel distinctively different from its
nearby competition.

Design Pasanella & Klein Stolzman & Berg
Architects
Project Mansfield Hotel
NEW YORK, NEW YORK

The Penthouse suites' earlier loft and living areas
were renovated to become an upscale two-level
suite.

PHOTO: MICHAEL MORAN

51

Design Wimberly Allison Tong & Goo
Architects and Planners
Project Hyatt Regency Coolum
QUEENSLAND, AUSTRALIA

PHOTO: HOWARD WOLFF

Design Hirsh Bedner & Associates
Architect Sydney C.L. Char, Wimberly Allison
Tong & Goo; Naokazu Hanadoh and Kazubiko
Kuroka, Shimizu Corp.
Lighting Jeff Miller
Project Grand Hyatt Bali
BALI, INDONESIA

The architects wanted a design that fit unobtrusively into the fragile environment of the island of Bali, and were inspired by the Balinese village. Buildings with courtyards were decentralized for an intimate setting. In this down view through the entry colonades, luminaires atop the columns provide a soft fill light, in keeping with the intimate atmosphere. The reception building is designed to resemble a Balinese water palace.

PHOTO: DONNA DAY

Design Di Leonardo International, Inc.
Project The New World Hotel,
Registration Desk
KOWLOON, HONG KONG

Some "fun" was created in the design, yet at a level where it maintained a high degree of sophistication.

53

Design Knauer Inc.
Project Milwaukee Hilton
MILWAUKEE, WISCONSIN

Designed in 1928 in the Empire style by Holabird
and Roche, the Milwaukee Hilton had suffered
years of neglect. When Knauer, Inc., stepped in to
reclaim the landmark hotel, they improved traffic
patterns in the lobby, without sacrificing any of the
original architectural details. Gold and silver leaf
highlight the lobby's Art Deco motif, as do period
fabrics, furnishings, and the original marble floors.

PHOTO: JAMES YOCHUM

Design Mithun Partners
Project Salish Lodge Spa Addition
SNOQUALIMIE, WASHINGTON

This intimate mountain retreat rests at the crest
of a 270-foot waterfall at the beginning of
the Cascades. The shingle-style architectural
character of the Spa addition is in keeping with
the original architecture of the Salish Lodge
designed by Mithun Partners nearly a decade
ago. The scale and the character of the spaces,
a warm Northwest palette of natural materials,
and a country inn appearance foster a peaceful
retreat.

Design Knauer, Inc.
Project Grand Geneva Resort And Spa
LAKE GENEVA, WISCONSIN

Along with other additions, a number of guest
rooms were reconfigured to create suites.

PHOTO: JAMES YOCHUM

Design AiGroup/Architects, P.C.
Project Radisson Plaza Hotel at Kalamazoo
Center, The Upjohn Suite Bath
KALAMAZOO, MICHIGAN

Created for the exclusive use of prominent exec-
utives, this comfortable bath features warm rich
marbles, brass appointments and a Jacuzzi bath
adjacent to the high style master bedroom.

PHOTO: GARY KNIGHT & ASSOCIATES

Design Knauer, Inc.
Project Grand Geneva Resort And Spa
LAKE GENEVA, WISCONSIN

Along with other additions, a number of guest
rooms were reconfigured to create suites.

PHOTO: JAMES YOCHUM

Design Mithun Partners
Project Salish Lodge Spa Addition
SNOQUALIMIE, WASHINGTON

The combination of indigenous materials with
Japanese references and forms captures the
essence of a sanctuary.

Design Knauer, Inc.
Project Grand Geneva Resort And Spa
LAKE GENEVA, WISCONSIN

A wellness spa was added to the resort.

PHOTO: JAMES YOCHUM

Design Studio Sofield, Inc.
Project Soho Grand
NEW YORK, NEW YORK

The historical, industrial theme is referred to throughout. Even the contemporary elegance of the guest rooms is punctuated with Stickley-era type furniture and furnishings.

Design Di Leonardo International, Inc.
Project Stouffers Concourse Hotel
ATLANTA, GEORGIA

Guestrooms were designed with traditional style and twenty-first-century comfort in mind.

PHOTO: JAIME ARDILES, ARCE

Design Design Continuum, Inc.
Project Hotel Inter-Continental
TORONTO, CANADA

The sophisticated club ambiance of the 211-room
Hotel Inter-Continental Toronto is derived from
warm wood tones, sparkling brass and crystal,
cool marble floors, walls and accents, and colors
of rose and moss green. This rich warmth
washes the hotel interiors from the lobby to
the guest rooms.

PHOTO: ROBERT MILLER

Design Vivian Nichols Associates, Inc.
Project Westchase Hilton Hotel,
typical guestroom
HOUSTON, TEXAS

Design Aiello Associates, Inc.
Project Westin Hotel Tabot Center, Suite
DENVER, COLORADO

PHOTO: DEAN J. BIRINYI

Design Birch Coffey Design Associates, Inc.
Project The Mercury

Design Media Five Limited
Project The Hyatt Regency
TUMON BAY, GUAM

The varied interiors of the Hyatt Regency Guam
present strong architectural statements with a
contemporary and exciting look.

PHOTO: MANNY HABRON, RON STARR

Design Aiello Associates, Inc.
Project Bullwhackers Gaming Establishment
CENTRAL CITY, COLORADO

Restaurant entry and view of custom mural by
Carlo Marchiori featuring and "opera goat"
theme.

PHOTO: ED LACASSE

Design PMG Architects
Project Delano Hotel
MIAMI BEACH, FLORIDA

Instead of the expected hotel lobby, Delano's
front door opens onto a multi-faceted indoor/
outdoor lobby comprised of eight distinct areas,
with no formal definitions to separate them.
Dramatic and quiet resting spots are included
along with places to eat, such as the Rose Bar
and the Breakfast Room.

PHOTO: COURTESY OF DELANO HOTEL

Design Barry Design Associates, Inc.
Project Imeperial Hotel Osaka
OSAKA, JAPAN

Western design was incorporated into many of the public spaces. Guests can even arrange to hold their nuptials in the Wedding Chapel.

Design Vivian/Nichols Associates, Inc.
Project Houstonian Hotel and Conference Center
HOUSTON, TEXAS

A reference to the atmosphere of a turn-of-the-century great lodge creates an understated mountain environment, replete with natural materials, warm colors, and commissioned nature and country artwork at the Houstonian Hotel and Conference Center.

PHOTO: MICHAEL FRENCE

Design Media Five Limited
Project The Hyatt Regency
TUMON BAY, GUAM

The varied interiors of the Hyatt Regency Guam present strong architectural statements with a contemporary and exciting look.

PHOTO: MANNY HABRON, RON STARR

Design Hughes Design Associates
Project Four Seasons Hotel
PHILADELPHIA, PENNSYLVANIA

The updated lobby and guest rooms of the Four Seasons Hotel, Philadelphia, are elegantly appointed with rich textiles and furnishings.

Design Dow/Fletcher
Project Portofino Inn at the Marina, Lobby
REDONDO BEACH, CALIFORNIA

Design Einhorn Yaffee Prescott Architecture and Engineering
Project The Equinox
MANCHESTER, VERMONT

Like the moldings, mantels, paneling, arches, and ceilings, the wooden stairways were meticulously restored.

PHOTO: BILL MURPHY

Design Brennan Beer Gorman/Architects
Brennan Beer Gorman Monk/Interiors
Project Crowne Plaza
WASHINGTON, D.C.

The hotel's expansion to 318 guest rooms was made possible by a new, two-story addition, accommodating forty Club-level rooms and a lounge. The architects employed a light-weight steel system for the expansion so that the structure of the vintage building would not be overpowered.

PHOTO: DAN CUNNINGHAM

Design Design Continuum, Inc.
Project Hotel Inter-Continental
TORONTO, CANADA

The sophisticated club ambiance of the 211-room Hotel Inter-Continental Toronto is derived from warm wood tones, sparkling brass and crystal, cool marble floors, walls and accents, and colors of rose and moss green. This rich warmth washes the hotel interiors from the lobby to the guest rooms.

PHOTO: ROBERT MILLER

Design AiGroup/Architects, P.C.
Project The Suite Hotel at Underground Atlanta, Standard Suite
ATLANTA, GEORGIA

Soothing tones of green and rose are accented with the warmth of the rich mahogany casegoods. Commissioned artwork designed especially for each room complements the relaxing residential atmosphere.

PHOTO: GARY KNIGHT & ASSOCIATES

Design Texeira, Inc.
Project Regent Beverly Wilshire
BEVERLY HILLS, CALIFORNIA

Design Texeira, Inc.
Project Regent Beverly Wilshire
BEVERLY HILLS, CALIFORNIA

Design Hill/Glazier Architects
Project Hualalai Four Seasons Resort
KONA, HAWAII

Hotel and bungalow forms are varied, creating unexpected discovery around every bend at Hualala.

Design Parisi
Project Mr. Woodson Golf Club House
RAMONA, CALIFORNIA

The design of the Mt. Woodson Hospitality Center was inspired by its historical site.

PHOTO: ED GOHLICH

Design Aiello Associates, Inc.
Project Westin Hotel Tabor Center,
Main Ballroom
DENVER, COLORADO

PHOTO: PHILLIP NILSSON

Design Aiello Associates, Inc.
Project Westin Hotel Tabor Center,
Typical Guest Room
DENVER, COLORADO

PHOTO: PHILLIP NILSSON

Design PMG Architects
Project Delano Hotel
MIAMI BEACH, FLORIDA

Outdoor eating areas in the orchard continue
the theme of the indoor/outdoor lobby.

PHOTO: COURTESY OF DELANO HOTEL

Design Pamela Temples Interiors, Inc.
Project Bluebeard's Tower
ST. THOMAS

Bluebeard's Tower, which dates back to the
1600's is one of St. Thomas' oldest structures. It
was successfully incorporated into a hotel in the
1930s.

PHOTO: MICHAEL LOWRY PHOTOGRAPHY &
ROBERT STARLING PHOTOGRAPHY

Design PMG Architects
Project Delano Hotel
MIAMI BEACH, FLORIDA

Instead of the expected hotel lobby, Delano's front
door opens onto a multi-faceted indoor/outdoor
lobby comprised of eight distinct areas, with no
formal definitions to separate them. Dramatic and
quiet resting spots are included along with places
to eat, such as the Rose Bar and the Breakfast
Room.

PHOTO: COURTESY OF DELANO HOTEL

Design Di Leonardo International, Inc.
Project The Westin Hotel
PROVIDENCE, RHODE ISLAND

The Westin Hotel in Providence, Rhode Island, serves as a major business convention center for this area of New England. The Rotunda lobby and Main lobby stairs are graced with Corinthian-style columns, all inspired by the impressive architectural history of Rhode Island.

PHOTO: WARREN JAGGER

Design Parisi
Project Big Horn Golf Resort, Palobrea
Hospitality Residences
PALM DESERT, CALIFORNIA

A warm and sophisticated desert ambiance greets guests at the Palobrea Hospitality Residences at Big Horn Golf Resort.

PHOTO: ED GOHLICH

Design Cheryl Rowley Interior Design
Project Beverly Prescott Hotel
LOS ANGELES, CALIFORNIA

PHOTO: COURTESY OF CHERYL ROWLEY INTERIOR

Design Di Leonardo International, Inc.
Project Stouffers Concourse Hotel
ATLANTA, GEORGIA

Stouffers Concourse Hotel at Hartsfield
International Airport, Atlanta, Georgia, with its
atrium garden court and private dining areas, is
helping to create a new traditional style for
Southern hospitality.

PHOTO: JAIME ARDILES, ARCE